Kids love reading
Choose Your Own Adventure®!

"These books are like games. Sometimes the choice seems like it will solve everything, but you wonder if it's a trap."

Matt Harmon, age 11

"I think you'd call this a book for active readers, and I am definitely an active reader!"

Ava Kendrick, age 11

"You decide your own fate, but your fate is still a surprise."

Chun Tao Lin, age 10

"Come on in this book if you're crazy enough! One wrong move and you're a goner!"

Ben Curley, age 9

"You can read *Choose Your Own Adventure* books so many wonderful ways. You could go find your dog or follow a unicorn."

Celia Lawton, 11

CHOOSE YOUR OWN ADVENTURE®

NIGHTMARE

SNAKE INVASION

BY DOUG WILHELM

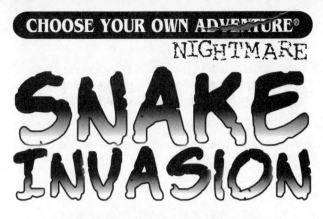

ILLUSTRATED BY VLADIMIR SEMIONOV
COVER ILLUSTRATED BY GABHOR UTOMO

CHOOSECO
WAITSFIELD, VERMONT

Snake Invasion artwork, design, and revised text
©2016 Chooseco LLC, Waitsfield, Vermont.
All Rights Reserved.

Illustrated by: Vladimir Semionov
Cover illustrated by: Gabhor Utomo
Book design: Stacey Boyd

For information regarding permission, write to:

CHOOSECO
P.O. Box 46
Waitsfield, Vermont 05673
www.cyoa.com

ISBN 10 1-937133-52-4
ISBN 13 978-1-937133-52-8

Published simultaneously in the United States and Canada

Printed in Canada

9 8 7 6 5 4 3 2 1

For Oliver Oparowski.
Musician. Reader. Cool kid.

BEWARE and WARNING!

This book is different from other books.

You and YOU ALONE are in charge of what happens in this story.

There are dangers, choices, adventures, and consequences. YOU must use all of your wits and much of your keen intelligence. The wrong decision could end in disaster—even death. But, don't despair. At any time, YOU can go back and make another choice, alter the path of your story, and change its result.

You and your family have just moved into a brand-new neighborhood at the edge of the Florida Everglades. Last week a guide came to your school to give a talk about the enormous Burmese pythons that are taking over the mysterious wetland, which seems really exciting—until your dog Zelda goes missing! Other pets in the neighborhood have been disappearing lately, and your best guess is that they're becoming something's dinner. You've been told *never* to step foot into the Everglades, full of alligators and ghostly legends, not to mention giant snakes. When you and your best friend, Jackson, throw caution to the wind what you find you could have never imagined. Will you make it out of the wetland alive?

These pythons have no natural enemies, and they eat almost *everything*.

There's a pounding on your front door.

You're expecting Jackson—he's your friend who comes over to play video games after school. But this isn't a "here I am, power up Battle Zone!" sort of knock. This is a fast-pounding, *"Open up quick!"* knock.

It's Jack and he's breathing hard. He looks panicked, and he's dumped his bike on your lawn. Spotting that, you feel a prickle of worry.

Your dad is super-strict. If he sees any digs in the grass, he'll get really upset. He keeps saying it's hard enough to keep a lawn alive, with the heat and the weird bugs in your brand-new neighborhood at the edge of the Everglades, Florida's gigantic, mysterious wetland.

But Jackson knocks that worry out of your mind.

Breathlessly, he wheezes: "Your dog!"

Then he shouts it. "Your *dog*!"

Turn to page 3.

"What?" you say. "She's in the backyard."

Jack shakes his head. He really likes little Zelda. Every time he comes over, he stops by your backyard first to say hello. An invisible fence keeps her in the yard. Zelda likes Jack, too. After he leaves her, she always yaps and yaps.

You realize something.

Zelda isn't yapping.

"Dude, she's not there any more!" Jack says. His eyes are wide and scared. "There was this...I couldn't believe it! It was huge!"

"What was huge?"

"The *snake!*"

Turn to the next page.

4

"Jack," you say, "what happened?"

"It's like ten feet long—I swear!" he gasps. "It carried her away in its mouth! I think it's going for the water. Come on—we have to *stop* it before it gets away with her. Come *on*!"

You glance backward toward the kitchen. You and your little sister have an after-school babysitter who drives you crazy. You're way too old for a *baby*sitter.

Every afternoon, every other week when you're with your dad, Julianna is here, making dinner. That's the worst part—she's a nut about weird, "healthy" foods.

Here she is now.

"What's all this *shouting*?" Julianna asks.

She's munching a carrot stick, one of her more normal foods. In her hand is a wooden spoon. She's probably been mixing up some lentil-kale-tofu-seaweed...thing.

"Uh...nothing. It's nothing," you say. "Jack's a little wound up, that's all. We need to step outside. To talk."

You push Jack back out the front door and follow.

Turn to page 6.

6

You shut the door behind you so Julianna won't hear. She likes to make "reports" to your dad—*really* helpful.

"Let's go," Jack says. "We have to move fast!"

"Um...*how* big did you say this snake is?"

"Like ten feet. At *least*," he says. "It's one of those pythons, like in that video. Remember?"

You remember very well. Last week an Everglades guide came to your school and gave a talk with scary videos about the enormous Burmese pythons that are overrunning the huge wetland.

Many Floridians bought the baby snakes as pets, but when the creatures started growing really big, lots of people let their pets loose at the edge of the Everglades.

Other pythons were liberated when hurricanes—which have been happening more and more often—wrecked roadside attractions like "Florida Reptile World" and "Gators and Snakes!"

The Burmese python is not a Florida native. It's an invasive species, and it has no natural enemies here. Fully grown, the snakes average ten to fifteen feet long.

By now, the expert said, there may be a quarter million of them in the Everglades. They eat almost *everything*.

Go on to the next page.

Your dog has been traveling with you and your sister from your mom's house to your dad's since they got divorced two years ago. For your little sister especially, Zelda has been the one thing she could hold onto.

"Come *on*!" Jack's almost frantic. "Got a baseball bat?"

"Sure, in the garage."

"Then go grab it!"

But you're thinking: *a ten-foot snake?* Your mind is working fast.

"I should call my dad at work," you say. "He'll call the cops, or Animal Rescue."

"Too slow," Jack says, shaking his head. "But *you* could call Animal Rescue—they'll know what to do. Look under Emergency Numbers. Front of the phone book."

Your friend turns to go. "That snake left a trail in the grass. I'm going to go chase it," he says. "We have to *move*!"

Turn to the next page.

You imagine the muscular predator making for the swamp, Zelda squirming in its jaws. You should go after it with Jack, right?

The Everglades guide said pythons aren't poisonous. They swallow their prey whole, but slowly. If you can catch the snake and bash it with the bat, maybe it will let Zelda go.

But you've both been told never, *ever* to step into the watery expanse beyond your backyard. Right back there is the Everglades—home of alligators, ghostly legends, *and* those monstrous snakes.

What hope could two kids have of stopping a hungry ten-foot python?

Maybe you'd better call Animal Rescue right now, while Jack tracks the animal.

But what if Jack goes into the wetland alone? He's so wound up, he just might.

You're torn and confused.

"Come *on*," Jack says. "Decide!"

If you grab the bat and go with Jack, turn to page 9.

If you call Animal Rescue while Jack tracks the snake, turn to page 66.

Clutching the bat, you follow Jack as he tears around the side of your house.

Where Zelda should be, the backyard is empty.

Jack points at the grass. "See?"

There's a faint, dry trail. It's a little wavy, like something very heavy slithered across the grass.

You follow the track onto your neighbor's yard, then across to another. All of these backyards are short, with trees here and there. The faint trail turns down a little slope. At the water's edge, it ends.

Turn to page 11.

You two stand there breathing hard. Your neighborhood's backyard shoreline is a little curvy, but everywhere the grass ends at the water. You've only lived in this neighborhood for a few months, but Jack remembers when this hadn't yet been filled in and was all wetlands.

As far as you can see, the Everglades are a widespread vista of shallow, sun-struck water and wavy grass. A few humps or clumps are out there too, like tree-capped islands.

"The water's not deep at all," Jack tells you. "There are a few channels, but that guide said the whole thing's a huge, shallow river. Incredibly wide."

You nod. "A river of grass," you say, remembering.

"We could *try* to look for Zelda," Jack says, taking a step toward the water.

You shake your head.

"It's hopeless," you whisper.

Turn to the next page.

The man who gave the snake talk at your school has an airboat tour business out on an old highway not far from your neighborhood. He told your class that the pythons who've escaped into the Glades can grow to be fifteen, even twenty feet long. They are naturally camouflaged, usually tan with big dark-brown patches.

The snake that took Zelda could be anywhere, slithering somewhere through the grass that seems to wave slightly in the breeze out there. *Sawgrass*, the guy called it.

"She's gone," you whisper.

Jack winces. "Those snakes eat bigger animals, too," he says. "Remember what that guy said, how they kill their prey? What's that word?"

"Constrict," you say. "They're from the same family as boa constrictors. They hold their prey tight with their front teeth, then wrap around and squeeze. And squeeze. 'Til you suffocate."

"Ugh," Jack says. "What a way to die."

You shudder.

Go on to the next page.

That night you have the awful job of telling your family what happened. Your sister cries for hours, long after you've both gone to bed. You lie there listening to her. All you can do is wish you could have somehow saved the pet she loved so much.

In the morning, walking your sister to meet the school bus, you see a flyer tacked to a telephone pole.

Missing: beloved cat. Small with gray stripes. Reward for *any* information!

There's a phone number.

As you save the number in your phone, a chill runs up your spine.

Turn to the next page.

14

When Jack joins you on the school bus, you tell him about the flyer. He gets really excited.

"We *know* something. We could get the reward!"

"For what," you say, "crushing someone's hope that their pet is still alive?"

"Let's go see that guide," Jack says. "He knows about snakes *and* the Everglades. Maybe he'll help us."

Go on to the next page.

You shake your head. "Something weird is happening. Two pets disappearing at the same time, from the same neighborhood? That's not normal."

"Right! So we investigate," Jack says. "First, let's call the number on that flyer. We'll find out what they know."

You still don't want to break a pet owner's heart by telling them what *you* know. You do want to solve the mystery—before another pet gets taken.

*If you go visit the Everglades guide,
turn to page 17.*

*If you call about the missing cat,
turn to page 57.*

16

You and Jack run to the tree, but you can't see what's happening. The moonlight illuminates the yard, but the leaves in the tree block your view.

"I'm going up there," you whisper to Jack.

"What? Are you *crazy*?"

You love climbing trees. In your old neighborhood, you were really good at it. You feel like you've got to see the snake in action.

"I know you're good at climbing," Jack whispers urgently, "but that thing's better. Did you see how *fast* it went up?"

You did. You're fascinated. "I just want to get to that first branch," you say. "I can see better from there."

"But we promised Ed we'd just watch," Jack reminds you.

"I won't interfere," you say. "I just want to see."

"Don't be stupid," Jack whispers. "*Don't*."

You bend your knees below the first branch. With one good jump, you could grab it and pull yourself up. But should you?

From up there you hear a terrified squeak. Has the predator caught the cat?

If you climb the tree, turn to page 22.

If you stay on the ground, turn to page 28.

You locate the number for Airboat Ed's Real Glades Tours on your phone and click to call.

Ed is friendly. "Happy to take you out," he says. "It's twenty-five dollars per person for a half-hour tour."

"Twenty-five bucks *each?*"

"Sure," he says. "Airboats have airplane engines. They use up a lot of gas."

You swallow hard. "Could we just ask you a question? You visited our school last week."

"Sure, I remember," he says. "Ask away."

So you tell him about the snake taking Zelda. He grunts like he's not surprised.

You mention the missing cat. He grunts again.

"Don't you think that's weird?" you ask. "Could the two things be connected?"

"Everything's connected," Airboat Ed says mysteriously.

There's a long pause. Finally he says, "There's actually something I need help with. If you kids will do a favor for me, I'll take you out on the Glades in the airboat. For free."

Turn to the next page.

18

You agree to do what Airboat Ed wants. At midnight that night, you grab your dad's police-model flashlight and sneak out to meet Jackson.

He's already in your backyard, standing under a palm tree. The light of a full moon softly bathes the yard.

"This better be worth it," you whisper as you approach him.

"Hey," Jack says, "a free airboat ride for a couple of hours standing around? That's easy."

You swallow hard, hoping he's right.

All Ed asked was that you two stand watch out here. He wants you to observe quietly in the dark, for two hours—then let him know what you see.

If you see anything.

He didn't explain why.

"Check your light," Jack says.

You flick the switch and the intense white beam startles you both. Switching it off, you glance back at your house to see if you woke anyone. But no lights come on.

You start to sit. Jack holds up his hand. "Don't sit down," he says.

"Why not?"

"Red ants—a Florida specialty. They'll sting you bad."

"So we have to *stand* here? For two hours?"

Jack shrugs. "Free airboat ride," he reminds you.

Turn to page 20.

20

For a long while, nothing happens. Out beyond your little yard, moonlight glints off watery patches among the sawgrass. Looking to the side, you see a cat. It roams silently across the backyard next to yours.

And then something *does* happen.

As the cat investigates something in the grass, you spot what looks like…yes, it is.

It's the head of a snake. It's a big head, poking silently above the short bank at the back of your neighbor's lawn. You jab Jack, and point. When he sees it, he mouths the word "Whoa."

Go on to the next page.

You two watch as the snake slithers soundlessly up from the water onto the lawn. It's moving toward the unsuspecting pet. You want to shout, "*Look out!*"—but you don't.

You promised Ed you would only watch. "If anything happens," he said, "you just eyeball it and tell me later."

Plus, if you make any noise you'll get caught out here. Your dad would be enraged. You just stand there, frozen, as the snake moves slowly toward its prey.

At the last second, the cat looks up, spots the predator—and zips up a branchy oak tree.

The snake slithers right up after it!

Turn to page 16.

22

"Give me the light," you say. Jack sighs, and hands it over.

You stick the flashlight into the back of your jeans, so your belt holds it, and with one quick jump, you grab the lowest branch. You walk your feet up the trunk and swing yourself onto the heavy branch.

Up in the leaves, it seems safer to switch on the light. When you do, you're shocked to see how close the snake is. It's just one branch above—and it has the cat in its jaws.

Reacting to the light, the snake lurches for the trunk to climb higher. Its sudden movement startles you, and you grab at the branch above for support. Your hand lands on something thick and fast-sliding—more of the snake! In horror, you rear back.

Now you've dropped the light and you're grabbing wildly—but there's nothing to grab.

Arms flailing, you're falling.

Turn to page 24.

24

You hit the ground hard and something snaps. Your collarbone is broken—you know it even before the sharp pain hits you.

You yell for Jackson, but he's nowhere nearby.

You can only lie there, confused and in stabbing pain. Strange sounds emerge from the watery swamp. The huge snake slithers down the tree. It has the house cat clutched in its wide-stretched jaws.

The poor cat's eyes are frozen in terror. So are you.

The predator glides by you. You watch it cross the backyard and slip down the little bank. The water gives a soft little *gulp* as the snake slips in.

Lying here wondering why Jack left, you feel very sleepy.

Go on to the next page.

There's another snake. Raising your head, you can see—it's crossing the neighbor's yard.

And there's another one!

Could this be a dream? A hallucination caused by pain and shock?

Maybe...but it feels very real. Two more snakes emerge from the swamp and glide across the backyards. It's almost like they're...

Hunting.

Now it hits you. That's exactly what they're doing.

They're *hunting*.

You want to scream, for help or just in terror. You're in shock from the injury. Your mouth is bone-dry and you feel like you might pass out.

In the distance, you hear a siren.

Turn to the next page.

Jack reappears, dashing around the side of your house.

"I ran home and called for help," he says, panting hard. "Are you okay?"

All you can do is gasp out, "Snakes! Snakes!"

Jack kneels. "Hey, it's okay," he says. "Hear that? The ambulance is coming."

The siren is coming closer.

Now lights switch on in your house.

With the one arm you can lift, you grab Jack's elbow.

"Snakes! It's an invasion!"

"It's okay," he says. "Try to relax. It's okay."

"But..."

Go on to the next page.

The ambulance crew arrives just before your dad comes bursting out of the back door. As adults surround you on the ground, you keep trying to warn everyone, but they just think you're delirious from the pain and shock.

The lights they're shining on you make it impossible for anyone to see beyond the crowd of people crouching around you. Only you know that beyond, in that darkness, giant predatory reptiles are slithering onto backyards.

Hunting for prey.

That is, *if* you saw what you think you saw.

You're sure it wasn't a dream or a hallucination— at least, you're pretty sure. But before you can tell anyone, a crew member speaks to you soothingly.

"I'm just going to give you something for the pain," she says. She rubs something cold on your good arm. You feel a little sting as she pokes in a needle.

You're *trying* to warn her that the huge snakes are just feet away from you, but now you can't seem to get words out. Inside you feel cold. You're sleepy, slipping off.

Before you lose consciousness, your last thought is: *No one will ever believe me. But I saw what I saw.*

The End

Jack's right. Climbing the tree, even a little ways, would only be asking for trouble. You and Jack get as close to the tree as possible, and wait in silence.

There's quick movement in the tree, then the gigantic snake slides down its trunk. Gripped in its wide-open jaws is a pale-yellow cat. The wide-eyed pet is frozen in terror.

You shudder as you watch the snake slither down onto the ground with its dinner. It moves toward the water—and now Jack snaps.

"No way," he says. "I'm *not* just watching this happen."

He strides across the lawn, holding the heavy police flashlight like a club.

"Whoa, Jackson," you say. "Wait!"

But it's too late.

At the edge of your yard, the snake slides down the short bank—and Jack chases it! He splashes into the water.

You have a bad feeling about this! The huge wetland has no paths, and Jack could get lost easily. Even if you two can catch that snake, what could you really do?

With alligators, snakes, and who knows what else out there, how much danger could you be getting into?

If you go into the water after Jack,
turn to page 68.

If you run inside to get help, turn to page 130.

In a few minutes you're pounding, dripping wet, on your dad's bedroom door.

"Dad! Dad! We need *help!*"

Your dad rushes you both into the car and tears off to the hospital. You're in the passenger seat and Jack's in the back. You're both soaked, your legs streaky with thin veins of now-dried blood.

"What in the *world* were you two doing?" your dad asks.

"Just…wading!" you say. "Are we gonna die?"

Your dad looks at you, then at Jack through the rear view mirror. You can't tell what he is thinking.

"You say it doesn't hurt any more?" he asks.

"Not at all," Jack says.

"But maybe it could be, like, in our bloodstream?" you say.

Your dad glances over. "Are you dizzy? Do you feel strange?"

"No," you admit.

"So," he asks, "how come you're all cut up?"

"Um…the sawgrass," you say weakly.

"What? How far out there did you *go?*"

"Hey," Jack says. "Isn't that the hospital?" Just in time, too.

Your dad yanks the wheel and the car squeals through a hard left turn, entering the driveway for the Emergency Room.

Turn to the next page.

30

The doctor on duty can't find any bite marks on either your foot or Jack's. He steps back, looking at your legs.

"Why did you go out in the Everglades at night?" he asks.

"We were watching for snakes," Jack pipes up. "We saw one take a cat, from a backyard—so we chased it."

You shrug. Why not tell them *most* of the truth?

You two tell the doc and your dad what happened. Neither of you mentions the ghostly swimming figure, or Ed the guide.

"Well," the doc says, "I think I know what the bite was, anyway. It's called a gator bug. People get them wading in the Glades, sometimes. It hurts like crazy, then it goes away. I think you're both fine, but let's clean up those sawgrass cuts."

On the way home, you're thinking, *At least we get an airboat ride.*

But your dad says, "Oh, by the way—you're grounded for a month."

Turn to page 32.

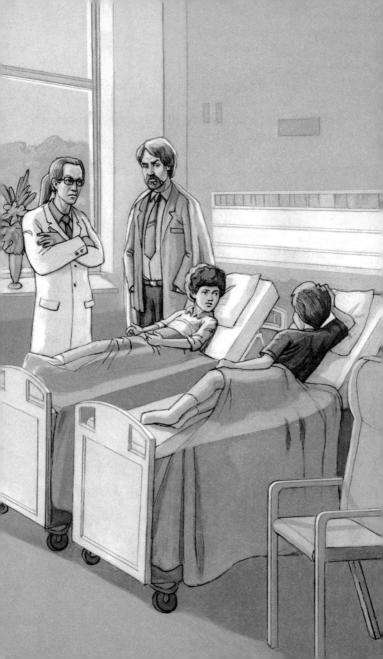

"A *month*?"

"Don't even *try* to argue," he says. "I'm sure your mom will back me up. Wading into the Everglades in the middle of the night? There's *no* explanation for that."

You look back at Jack. He shrugs.

You both know there's no point in saying anything about what you saw out there. You haven't even told Jack how the swimming boy seemed, somehow, to be leading you home. Even he might not believe that.

"The Everglades are way mysterious," you say.

"They're *dangerous*," your dad says. "Jack, I'm afraid we're going to have to tell your parents about this."

Jack groans. "I'll be grounded for a *year*," he says.

"Well," you say, resigned to your fate, "I guess it's better than dying from a snakebite."

Your dad shakes his head. "I don't want to hear another word," he says. "End of discussion."

You look back at Jack. He winks.

While you're stuck indoors these next few weeks, you two will have a lot to talk and text about—especially since you know you're the only ones who will ever believe what happened to you tonight.

The End

You and Jack bike to the boat access. This is where fishermen and other boaters back their trailers into the water. Today, the parking lot is quiet.

Channels have been cut to create safe paths for regular boats. Because the water is usually so shallow, only an airboat can safely traverse the Everglades.

From out on the water you hear a distinctive roar.

As you two stand on shore and watch, an airboat comes zooming toward you. It's an odd-looking craft, flat-bottomed with its pilot sitting atop a rickety-looking metal platform. Behind his platform is a very large propeller, in a big wire cage.

As the airboat slides to a stop, a wiry young man hops down from the pilot's chair.

"Tommy Osceola," he says, extending a hand. "You're the Disappearing Pet bloggers, right?"

"That's us," says Jack.

Tommy Osceola nods back at his boat. "Want to go for a short ride?"

Turn to page 35.

Next thing you know, you're flying through the Everglades, soaring across its shallows with the boat's engine roaring behind you. Tommy Osceola points out basking alligators, big and spiny-backed. Wide-winged birds lift up gracefully to wheel away from your noisy, careening craft.

Tommy steers toward one of the odd little islands that rise from these flat, grassy shallows. He cuts the engine as he glides in. In the sudden quiet, Tommy tells you this place—he calls it a hammock—is one of his clan's ancestral campgrounds.

"Your clan?" Jack asks.

"That's right," Tommy says. "We're Miccosukee. The first people of the Everglades."

"Is that like the Seminoles?"

"Different tribe," he says. "We're not as well-known 'cause nobody named any teams after us."

"That's too bad," Jack says.

Tommy smiles. "Not really."

He takes you on a quick tour of this tiny island, showing you its clean-swept areas for camping and campfires. You three sit down in the shade of an ancient-looking, wide-spreading tree.

"For centuries in the Everglades," Tommy tells you, "life was in balance. It's not any more."

Turn to page 53.

Jack rushes straight into the sawgrass.

"Ow!" he says. "These things are harsh!"

"That's what I was…"

"Wait!" he says. "Where'd it go?"

You both stand looking around. There's no sign of the swimming apparition.

"That's it," you say, "we're heading back."

Jack's scream cuts you off, and he leaps up out of the water.

Go on to the next page.

Jack hops up and down on one foot. "Something *bit* me," he gasps out.

Your friend falls hard against you. You stagger back—and now a stabbing, shrieking pain soars up from your foot.

"OW! OWWW!!!"

The pain shooting up your own leg is so strong that you feel dizzy. "Something got me too!" you scream. "It really *hurts*!"

Jack is perching on one leg like a wading bird, holding his foot. "I can't see…is there a bite mark?"

You try to peer at his dripping foot, but your own pain is almost blinding. Could a snake have bitten you both?

What was it the Everglades guide said? There are several kinds of poisonous snakes in the Glades: water moccasins and two kinds of rattlesnakes.

Now the memory hits you so hard it penetrates the white-hot pain that's shooting up from your foot.

You can hear the guide as he says, "They can *all* strike in the water, those snakes. So be careful out there!"

Turn to the next page.

Your foot feels like it was stabbed.

If you were bitten by a water moccasin or a rattlesnake, you may have only minutes to get help. The same is true for Jack.

Jack tries to look at his foot again and loses his balance. With his arms flapping, he falls back and splashes. You reach down to pull him up...and as you do, you spot the boy, glowing just ahead in the water.

The boy swims backward out of the sawgrass. Even as you shiver in pain and terror, you swear that the figure, even though it's still a few inches under the water, is waving.

Maybe it's swimming, maybe it's waving, or maybe both—you'll never know. But some deep instinct tells you it doesn't mean you harm.

The boy continues his ghostly, slow backstroke. It's moving, under the water, toward the sawgrass again.

Something in you tells you to follow.

Go on to the next page.

Silently, the boy glides into the grass again, like the thick blades aren't even there. Trying to ignore your stabbing pain, you reach back and grab Jack's hand.

"Come on!" You get in Jack's face. "I got bit too, okay? But our only chance is to get back as fast as we can."

Turn to the next page.

40

In the moonlight, his face looks wild with fear, but he nods.

You both gather your courage, and push through the heavy thicket. Only you understand you are following the ghostly swimming boy. Jack is just stumbling along after you.

How many minutes do you have before the venom truly sets in?

Swimming beneath the water's surface, the glowing shape leads you through a last patch of sharp grass. Emerging, you carefully push the heavy blades aside—and there ahead, like a dream come true, is your neighborhood.

The houses are dark. You can make out trees standing here and there in the backyards.

You look back to the water. But the glowing boy has vanished.

Go on to the next page.

You stumble toward shore. Jack's right behind you, but he stops and stands still in the water.

"Hey," he says. "Hey! It doesn't hurt any more," he says.

Your leg still hurts fiercely, and you're impatient.

"Just come *on*," you say through teeth clenched tight against the pain. You take a few steps more, and *your* pain fades away.

"I don't hurt any more either," you tell Jack.

"So we're okay!" he says. "Let's go find that ghost thing. I want to *see* it again!"

You want to agree—you'd love to get another look at the swimming boy. But what if the snake venom has passed into your bloodstream, and *that's* why it stopped hurting?

If you think the bite was serious and you need to get help, turn to page 29.

If you decide the bite was nothing, turn to page 132.

42

You've chosen to stay.

"Be *very careful* with that thing," Tommy says, motioning to the gun in your hand. He shows you how to take the safety off—but he leaves it on when he hands it back to you.

You watch him push the skiff away with his pole. Jack sits in the bow

You're alone in the Everglades, late at night on a tiny island. This, you remember, is an ancient Indian campground. You can't help wondering: Is it haunted?

Whether it is or not, nothing happens for what seems like a long time. You hear strange sounds, and some are scary—shrieks, chatters, weird low grunts. But, you tell yourself, *it's only nature.* You recall what Tommy told you: "You are always the biggest creature out here. If not the biggest—the smartest."

As you sit on a rock in the open, something rustles in the underbrush. It's close by. And what happens next proves Tommy wrong.

You're *not* the biggest creature on this island.

Turn to page 44.

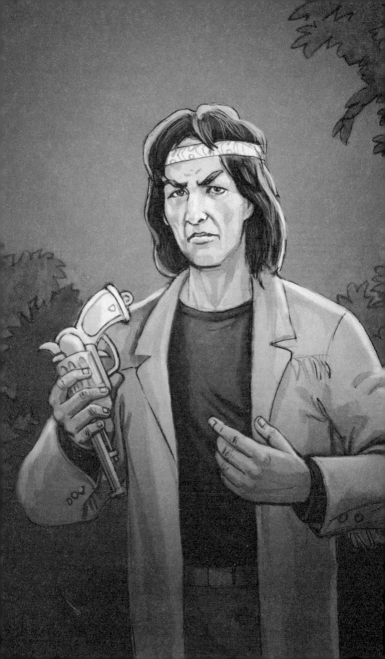

44

Over in some underbrush, the moonlight catches movement. Something dark is moving in there.

A raccoon? No…it's big.

It's *really* big.

As the thing pushes through the tangled vegetation, you make out a dark figure that rises to its full height.

It's the shape of a human being.

You rub your eyes, but the thing is still there. It has to be eight feet tall! And it looks to be covered in dark hair.

You stay absolutely motionless. The creature hasn't seen you yet…but it will.

As you try to make your brain work again, a horrible smell hits you. And you remember something.

Doing research for your blog project, you read stuff on the internet about a legendary creature, a Bigfoot of the Everglades. People swear this creature exists. There have been eyewitness sightings—but no one has ever found real proof.

Yet everyone who has come within a thousand feet of the manlike creature say that it stinks to high heaven. It smells, basically, like a sulfurous fart.

People call this creature the Skunk Ape. You're looking right at it…*and* smelling it.

Turn to page 65.

"Come on, Jack," you say firmly. "We're going back *now*."

"Aw, all right," he says. "But which way?"

Almost waist deep in water, you can't see over the sawgrass. Turning to look, you realize it's pretty much all around you, here.

You feel a new pang of deep fear. Thin veins of blood are running down your legs, and Jack's forearms are popping out with bloody pinpricks from pushing into the sawgrass. You've figured out how to move through the thickets of grass more gently, so you don't cut yourself up...but the damage is done.

You're both creating a trail of blood through the Everglades. It's leading right toward you.

Turn to page 48.

48

"I've got an idea," Jack says.

He bends at the knees, bracing himself, and cups his two hands down by the water.

"Step up here," he says. "Then you can see over that stuff."

When you try it, Jack holds you for a second, then staggers backward—and you both crash into the shallow water. Your brain flashes with the image of an alligator, jaws wide open, coming at you fast. Your panic makes you leap backward.

"We have to try again," you say urgently to Jack. "Quick!"

"Okay, okay," he says.

When you're up there again, teetering, you say, "Can you hold me?"

"For about two more seconds! What do you see?"

Looking this way then that, you only see darkness. All across the moonlit horizon, all you see are the blurry tops of sawgrasses and the shiny surface of water, broken here and there by what look like tree-topped islands.

You say, "Can you turn?"

"*Turn?*"

"Yeah—just so I can look the other way."

Please don't fall again, your brain pleads silently.

Go on to the next page.

Jackson staggers through a half-turn, splashing the water just enough to make you worry. Lights turn on, illuminating houses at the edge of the Glades. You recognize your *own* house lighting up from the inside. Soon someone will notice you're gone.

"Okay, I see it! Let me down, but—hey! Not like that!"

Too late: As Jack leans forward for some reason, you tilt and fall, face down. You hit the water with a sickening *splat.*

"What'd you do *that* for," you manage to gasp, when you've pulled yourself out of the now-mucky, stirred-up water.

"I don't know, I...oh no, oh no what's *that*?"

No more than five feet away in the water, a wet, black, spiny back glides by. Petrified, you freeze and hold your breath.

Turn to the next page.

50

And now it's gone.

"Th-th-that was an alligator," Jack stutters. "We have to get *out* of here!"

"I know! Follow me!"

You and Jack escape the sawgrass with relief. You've completed your mission for Ed, and the free airboat ride will be yours.

Go on to the next page.

"What do you guys think? Nice, huh?"

Airboat Ed is shouting from behind you in his tall pilot's chair. You and Jack are his only passengers, sitting on a bench on the airboat's deck as the wind whips through your hair. The flat-bottomed craft is powered by an aircraft engine. Its backward-facing propeller sends you across the shallow water like you're flying.

You told Ed how you chased the python but lost it in the sawgrass. You haven't mentioned the ghostly, swimming boy…at least, you haven't yet.

And Ed was as good as his promise. That's why you're out here two days later, the wind in your face and the engine's roar in your ears as Airboat Ed takes you on a trip into the largest wetland on the face of the earth.

Turn to the next page.

52

The Everglades, Ed says, cover nearly all of southern Florida, except for the coastlines. The water flows slowly through shallows that only allow airboats to pass through.

As Ed steers you past endless stretches of sawgrass, here and there you pass little islands that rise like humps, crested with oddly shaped trees.

Zipping by one island, you see its banks are blocked by the gray, tangled roots of mangrove trees.

"Do people *live* on the islands?" you shout up to Ed.

"The Seminoles and the Miccosukee used to," he calls back. "Those are the native people of the Glades. They call the islands hammocks. Want to visit one?"

"Sure!" Jack calls back.

Ed swerves the boat to the right. Big white wading birds rise up and wheel overhead.

The boat approaches a small bulge of land. One big tree spreads wide over much of it. Now you see a grassy beach. Ed cuts the engine and lets the airboat glide up, sliding to a stop.

"This is an old Seminole mound," Ed says as he climbs down. "Be respectful. Ancient spirits are here."

Turn to page 76.

"The Everglades used to cover nearly all of South Florida, except for the coasts," Tommy explains. "For eons, fresh water flowed slowly south, all across this landscape, like a wide, shallow river. That water used to be so clean—but not any more. Huge factory farms are polluting it. So are new housing subdivisions. Like yours."

"We're just kids!" you say.

"I know. It's not your fault," Tommy agrees. "But for years, developers have been filling in pieces of the wetland, to build houses they can sell to make money. Meanwhile, the government has dammed and channeled the water all over the place. It doesn't flow like it should any more."

Jack asks, "Are the snakes part of that? The pythons?"

Turn to the next page.

Tommy nods. "They're overrunning the Everglades: giant snakes that aren't from here, and that eat almost anything. They've been wiping out the small wild animals, the possums and raccoons and so forth, plus the eggs of the big birds.

"When all that food is gone," Tommy says, "we've been worried they'll start coming for pets. In all these new neighborhoods on the edge of the water, there's a lot of python prey."

Turn to page 56.

56

Tommy Osceola asks you to meet him back at the boat access tonight at midnight.

"Burmese pythons are nocturnal," he explains. "So are some of the shadier people around here."

Nervously, you both agree to sneak out and meet him. If you get caught, your parents will be beyond furious. But for some reason, you trust Tommy Osceola.

Just after midnight, you're back on the water—this time, in a flat-bottomed skiff that Tommy poles across the shallows to the island. The water shines in the light of a full moon.

"Okay. Here's the plan," he says when you reach the island. "There's a larger hammock, not far from here—and lately, something hasn't been right about that place. I want to check it out. I need one of you to come with me."

"We'll both come," Jack says, but Tommy shakes his head.

"I need one person to stay here, for emergency contact," he says. "If we get in trouble, we'll call you. Then you can call for help."

Tommy reaches into a gym bag he's taken from the boat, and pulls out a pistol. Jack's eyes get big.

"Whoever stays here," Tommy says, "I want you to take this. Just in case."

If you take the gun and stay,
turn to page 42.

If Jack stays and you go with Tommy,
turn to page 94.

When you call the number on the flyer after school, you tell the woman who answers that you're calling about her missing cat.

"Have you seen Velvet? Do you know where she is?"

"Well, not exactly," you stutter.

"Please tell me! If what you say leads to Velvet coming back to us unharmed, the reward is $500."

The number makes you jump. Then you realize what the woman just said.

"Um...did you say she has to come back to you unharmed? I mean, for the reward."

Turn to the next page.

58

"Yes, of course 'unharmed'!" says the woman.

You sigh. "I guess I can't really help you," you say.

"What? Why?" The woman sounds suspicious. "Did you *hurt* Velvet? I've got your number on caller ID—if you took our cat, I'm calling the police!"

"No no, please, it's nothing like that," you say quickly. "We're just two kids who kind of hoped we could find your cat. To help out. But...I really don't think we could.

"I'm sorry to bother you and all. I really hope you find your cat," you add before hanging up.

Now you feel terrible. You're pretty sure the woman will never find her cat—and you think you know why.

"Aw, man," Jack says when you tell him. "Five hundred bucks down the drain!"

"We should call Animal Rescue," you say. "Maybe these two cases aren't the only ones, you know?"

Jack's already got his phone out, doing a search. He reads out the phone number just as the school bus pulls up to your stop.

Turn to page 60.

Delia stares out at the Everglades, then turns to you two.

"We're going to need your help to spread the word," she says. "We need to alert everyone around here—and your blog can help. People are reading it."

"What about people's pets?" you ask. "Can you protect them?"

"We can tell everyone to keep their animals inside," she says, "but how can we stop those creatures? The State of Florida has organized big python hunts before. The snakes are so elusive, and so well-camouflaged, even the best hunters can hardly find any."

"Well," you say, "I think they've eaten all the wild animals out there, so now they're coming for the pets."

Soberly, Delia nods. She does believe you now.

Jack says, "Can *anyone* stop them?"

Turn to page 75.

60

When the white Animal Rescue van pulls into your driveway, you rush to meet it.

A young woman unfolds herself to step out. She has to be six and a half feet tall!

All in a rush, you two tell her what you think happened to Zelda.

"Hmm," she says, looking around. "Some small pets *have* begun disappearing from waterside properties like this."

"You mean, from all over?"

"I don't know about all over," she says. "I've just heard about a couple of pets disappearing from around here. This is a very big subdivision. Lots and lots of homes."

"And lots of pets," Jack adds.

The tall woman nods.

You ask, "Could it be…snakes?"

"Oh, that's highly unlikely," she says, waving the notion away. "We suspect pet-nappers."

"Why?"

"Well, purebred pets are very valuable."

"Zelda wasn't purebred," you tell her. "We got her from the pound."

The woman stiffens. She doesn't seem to like having her expertise questioned.

"We're not really a detective agency," she says, kind of coldly. "Sorry I can't help you more."

She wishes you luck, and drives away.

"Whoa," Jack says. "She wouldn't even *listen* to us!"

Turn to page 62.

You and Jack decide to create a blog, "The Disappearing Pets of Gladeview Meadows." You also put up old-fashioned flyers around the neighborhood:

Help us find the missing pets!

You get a couple of anguished phone calls, plus several comments on the blog. "Our little Jake was an outdoor cat," one comment says. "Now we can't find him anywhere."

"We let Zippy out one morning to do his business, like every morning," another writes. "But this time he didn't come back. He always came back!"

The local paper writes a very short article about your investigation. You get a few comments that are strange.

Someone writes, "No one is safe! They'll come for our children!"

Another says, "This is why every household should have assault weapons!"

You two wonder if you made a big mistake, getting involved in this mystery.

Then you get a phone call.

Go on to the next page.

"I know this part of the Glades as well as anyone alive," says a young-sounding guy on the phone. "My people have been here for centuries. I think you might have stumbled onto something big."

You gulp.

"You do?"

"It's very possible," he says. "Humans have put the ecology of the Everglades out of balance—and now some weird things are happening. I've been trying to tell people, but nobody will listen."

"I know the feeling," you say.

"But your blog is starting to get readers," he says. "If you'll work with me, we could *make* people pay attention."

"How?"

"Do you have a smartphone?"

"Well, sure," you say.

"Meet me tomorrow morning, at nine," the man says. "Do you know the boat access in Gladeview Acres?"

"Yeah. That's our neighborhood."

"Meet me there. Bring your phone."

"There's two of us," you say.

"Even better," he says. "Bring *two* phones."

Turn to the next page.

On Saturday morning, just as you're about to head out, your phone rings again.

"Hello," says a woman. Her voice sounds familiar. "I'm Delia Consul from Animal Rescue."

"Oh, right," you say. *You're the one who didn't believe us.*

"Are you the person who called from this number several days ago?" she asks. "It was about a missing dog."

"Yeah, that was me," you say. "Did you find Zelda?"

"No, but we've just had an emergency call from a house on your street," she says. "Something about snakes in her pet enclosure. The woman sounds elderly, and she's quite upset. I'm on my way, but I can't get there for maybe twenty minutes. I remember you talking about snakes—maybe you could run over and see what's happening?"

"Well…"

"Just try to calm her down," Delia says. "Until I can get there. We depend on help from volunteers."

Snakes in an enclosure? It sounds so bizarre it might be worth checking out. But you've just promised to meet the mystery man.

If you meet the man who wants to team up, turn to page 33.

If you check out the snake emergency, turn to page 80.

You could try to call Jack, and beg them to come back—but if you move, the creature's going to spot you.

It *will* spot you—any second. You've got to run for it.

You're about to make a mad dash for the water, thinking it's fatal even to try, when the Skunk Ape—if that's what it is—turns and ambles back into the underbrush.

As quietly as you possibly can, you start moving toward some tall grass on the side of the island away from the creature.

Gun in your hand, placing each foot down gently, you creep across the open ground.

You don't relax until you're pushing into the tall grass.

You step down a little slope. It's hard to see in here. As you place your right foot into what seems like a shallow hole, there's a rattling sound—and sharp movement all around your leg.

Something sharp strikes your ankle.

Turn to page 67.

Animal Rescue says they'll send someone right out.

"Zelda's *gone*," Jack shouts at you. "That snake's out there somewhere, and it's got her. This is *bad*!"

"Animal Rescue's on its way," you say. "Maybe they can do something."

"Like what? That thing probably has her half-swallowed already!"

Jack waves toward the vast, flat Everglades. Water shines in the sunlight, with great stretches of tall grass growing out of it, plus occasional bumps that look like tree-fringed islands.

"That guide said there's a million of those snakes out there," Jack says.

"He said a quarter million. Maybe."

"But they're *breeding*," Jack points out. "And they have no natural enemies. Who knows how many of them are really out there?"

"Maybe nobody knows for sure," you admit. "And they all need to eat."

Turn to page 60.

You've stepped into a nest of rattlesnakes.

Falling backward and dropping the pistol in terrified panic, you scramble away from the snake pit.

Back on open ground, the moonlight shows you two tiny holes in a soft part of your right ankle. *Snakebite.*

You're in terrible trouble.

"Help! Help, somebody!" You yell this as loud as you can. "Somebody, please help—*I don't want to die!*"

You hear something. The underbrush parts, and the ape runs into the open. You don't move. If you try to run away now, the venom will only spread more quickly into your system.

The Skunk Ape comes closer. He looks at you, tilting his head as if he's curious. He looks almost... like he wants to help.

You hold up your injured leg.

The creature comes closer. It bends, peers at your leg, and grunts. Now it kneels beside you. Its odor almost chokes you, but you no longer care.

In one giant hand, the Skunk Ape lifts your leg toward its great shaggy head. It bends closer, and sucks the rattlesnake venom from your leg.

Turn to page 93.

68

You kick off your flip-flops and step into the water that's gleaming with moonlight. It only comes up to your knees. Your feet hit slippery muck, but you are able to push along after your friend.

Jack plunges into the sawgrass. Seeing his shoulders and dark head bobbing about twenty feet ahead, you take a deep breath and push into the grass.

At that moment you realize why it's called *saw*grass. You feel a prickling all down your legs, like tiny stings. Looking down, you see tiny spots of blood emerging all down the front of your legs from your shorts to your knees.

The sawgrass—now you remember this, the guide told you at school—has microscopic teeth. If you push against the grass's triangular blades, or push through them like you're doing now, those teeth can speckle you with tiny punctures.

You shudder. You're knee-deep in water, leaking blood. How many Everglades creatures can smell that?

You can barely see Jack. You're already close to panic when something slides against your lower leg.

It's something thick...and snakelike.

Turn to page 70.

70

Recoiling, you hop backward with a splash. You can't see anything in the water. Taking a deep breath, you stumble forward, as fast as you can. You've got to get out of this nasty sharp grass!

You emerge into a wash of sawgrass-free moonlit water. Up ahead, Jack is gripping the flashlight, looking all around.

"I swear I was on its tail," he says.

He takes a step forward—and is pulled underwater.

Go on to the next page.

"Jack!"

You plunge toward where Jack thrashes in the water. Here it's darker, and looks deeper.

Looking around, you see channel markers. They've been placed to show where boats can pass, through this deeper path cut through the wetland. You don't see Jack.

Suddenly, he comes up flailing and gasping.

"Grab my hand, come on!" you say, reaching for his fingers. The flashlight falls into the murk. Jack slides back down into deep water and you lunge forward, grabbing him by the wrist.

You lean back and pull, forgetting everything else: the snake that slid past you underwater, the liquid seeping down your legs, even the fear of what might be attracted by the thick smell of blood.

You haul your friend over to the shallows. He sits there breathing hard in water up to his chest.

"Can you get up?" you ask. "We really should head back."

You look around, trying to spot some lights that'll tell you which way *is* back. But Jack's on his feet again—and he's pointing toward the deeper water.

"Wh...wh...*what* is that?" he asks.

You look to where Jack is pointing. And you see it too.

Turn to the next page.

72

A few feet away, over the edge in the channel, a large phosphorescent mass glows in the water.

You move along the edge of the shallows to get a better look.

It's a boy about your age. He's maybe a foot underwater. You can see his pale, silent, almost-glowing figure. He's face-up.

He's...*swimming*.

The boy's arms are slowly moving. His legs are moving too, like he's doing some ghostly backstroke. But he's *under* the water...and he's not coming up for breaths of air.

Turn to page 74.

The boy glides slowly away from you. As you both stand and watch, he slowly passes into the vegetation that grows up from the water, like the thick sawgrass isn't even there.

Now only his white-glowing legs are visible, scissoring slowly back and forth.

And now the boy has disappeared in the grass.

Jack's face is ghostly pale. His eyes are huge. "We should follow him," he says.

He starts to plunge toward the sawgrass—but you grab his t-shirt from behind.

"No, Jack," you say. "That grass is cutting us up—and we need to get back."

"I *have* to see if that's real or what," Jack says. "You coming?"

You really don't want to go with him. At the same time, you really do.

If you go with Jack, turn to page 36.

If you try to find your way home, turn to page 46.

"These snakes are an invasive species," says Delia. "They don't belong in the Everglades, and now they're out of control."

You glance up and down the long shoreline. You see backyard after backyard, home after home. In your neighborhood alone, hundreds of brand-new houses have been built here. All these people, like you and your family, have moved onto yet another filled-in piece of the once-wild Everglades.

"Maybe that's true of us, too," you say.

"Us who?" Jack asks.

"Us humans. Around here, maybe we're also an invasive species."

The three of you stand there, staring out across the water.

Nobody can think of anything to say.

The End

76

Ed's long, lean face is darkened and creased by years in the bright sun. As you three crouch under the wide-spreading shade of a Royal Poinciana tree, Ed digs into the ground with his Swiss Army knife. He pulls out a little bleached-white seashell.

"Believe it or not, this whole island is a mound of shells," Ed says. "That's pretty much what the hammocks are. This one was built up over centuries, by ancient tribal people. They ate the shellfish for food."

"That's incredible," says Jack.

You agree, then take a deep breath.

"Hey Ed," you say, "when Jack and I were out in the water that night...we saw something. We don't really know what it was."

Ed leans closer. "Tell me," he says.

Turn to page 78.

Ed listens as you and Jack describe the ghostly boy who seemed to swim slowly, on his back, just beneath the water. When you've told all that you can remember, he nods.

"I've heard about that," Ed says. "But you're the first ones I've met who *saw* it."

"What *was* it?" Jack asks.

Ed scratches at the ground with his knife. "Well, the story is that many years ago, some kids were out canoeing in that part of the Glades. It was night, but the moon was bright. Back then, the Everglades were huge and wild. This was before all the modern development carved up huge parts of them for houses and farms.

"As the story tells it," Ed says, "one of the boys got out of the canoe to go exploring in the shallows of the Glades. He waded off on his own, but he didn't see where the water dropped into a deep channel. And he couldn't swim.

"The boy's friends had paddled a ways ahead when they heard him yelling for help," Ed says. "They turned back and searched around frantically, but they couldn't find him.

"They looked everywhere. But he was gone."

Go on to the next page.

"The legend is that, for all these years," Ed says, "that boy's spirit has been searching through these waters. When the moon is full, he swims just under the surface."

"But why?" Jack asks.

Ed shrugs. "Many people believe the spirit needs to help someone. It searches and searches, just like the boy's friends searched for him. If it can find someone to help, maybe then the spirit will be released from its quest."

Ed looks up at you. "Like I told you, I've never yet met someone who actually *saw* the swimming boy. But you say he showed you how to get back home?"

"Yeah," you say.

"You never told me that part," Jack says.

"I didn't know if you'd believe me," you admit.

Ed peers closely at you two. Then he stares off across the Everglades.

"What I think," he finally says, "is that you two might have found a way to set the ghost of that poor kid free."

A chill runs shivering up your spine. You decide right then that you're going to learn everything you can about the Everglades—this immense, yet shrinking, home of gators, giant snakes, and incredible mysteries.

The End

80

You decide to check out Delia's "emergency." Jack thinks it sounds cool.

You're not so sure. "The snakes are probably the lady's pets," you say.

"Could be," he agrees, "but I can't stop thinking about that thing taking Zelda. What's the address for this place?"

It's just a few doors from your house. Jack says he'll beat you there, but you dash over and get there first.

An older woman answers the door. Her hair is white, and her eyes are wide with panic and fear.

"Are *you* Animal Rescue?" she asks.

"Not exactly—they'll be here in a few minutes," you say. "They asked my friend and me to come over as volunteers, because we're close. We've been working on the snake situation."

"Oh my gosh, then please come in!" she says. "I'm all alone here, except for my babies."

Turn to page 82.

82

The old woman leads you through her house, to a backyard patio. The yard is half filled with a very large pet enclosure. It has wire sides and top, and it's full of cats—plus three muscular, writhing Burmese pythons.

One of the big, brown-spotted snakes has a small cat captured in its jaws. The other two are slithering across the grass in there, while four or five frenzied cats—they're moving so quickly, it's hard to count—leap and dash around the pen.

As you watch, a small gray cat jumps high and clings with its claws to the wire siding. A python lunges at the pet with terrifying power. The gray cat squeals and leaps away, barely eluding the predator's jaws.

"Please! My kitties!" the elderly woman says. "You have to save them!"

Just then, Jack comes skittering around the corner. Staring open-mouthed at the pen and the wild activity inside, he drops his bike.

Quickly he unstraps his backpack. He pulls out the two aluminum baseball bats that are sticking up from the top.

"Let's get in there," he says.

Turn to page 84.

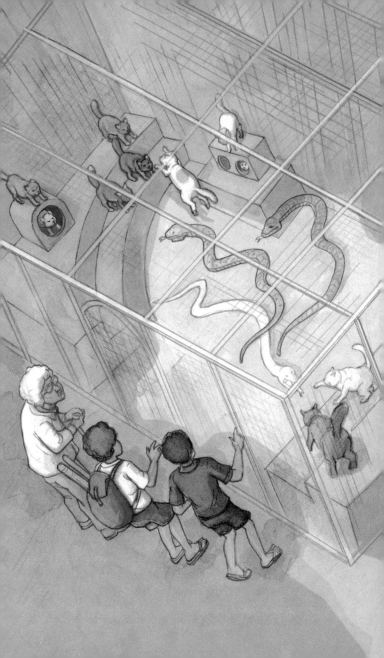

84

Into the *cage*? With three hungry pythons?

"Wait!" the woman says.

She dashes inside and returns with an air horn.

"I don't want you kids going inside the pen— maybe this will drive them off," she says. "But please save my babies!"

Undaunted, Jack goes to the gate of the pet enclosure. He's about to pull it open.

"How would you even swing a bat in there?" you ask.

"Watch me," Jack says.

The wire enclosure is big, but not quite high enough for you to stand inside. You think fast. If Jack does open the gate, maybe you can scare the snakes away with a blast from the horn. *Maybe.*

If you tell Jack to open the cage while you blast the horn, turn to page 85.

If you grab a bat to help Jack, turn to page 88.

You grab the air horn.

"Open the gate," you say to Jack, "then stand back."

"What?"

"I'll blast them away! It's worth a shot," you say.

Jack's reluctant, but he nods.

He fiddles with the latch, then releases it.

For the split-second before the gate swings open, you wonder how the snakes got *in*. Then you see a very small gap, at the base of the cage on this side. These are big, powerful creatures: they must have pushed their way under the big structure, just enough to lift it and get in.

As Jack swings open the gate, you push the air horn up against the wire.

When you push the button, an ear-shattering blast of sound hits the slithering, leaping, lunging creatures in there.

Turn to page 87.

The pythons couldn't care less about the air horn's blast.

The big snakes keep on twisting and sliding after the terrified cats. Even while your thumb is still pressed against the horn's red button, a snake lunges at an upper corner of the cage. The gray cat barely escapes, a second time.

You know the pets can't keep eluding these predators for much longer.

"That's it," Jack says, tossing you a bat. "I'm going in."

"Okay," you say. "Let's do this."

Turn to the next page.

88

Jack leaps into the cage. Bent at the waist, he swings his bat. It thuds against the muscular side of a python, but the snake doesn't react.

Jack is flailing his bat wildly. If you follow him in, you could get smacked.

The terrified cats burst through the open gate, and run scattering across the lawn. Two pythons emerge to pursue them. Their thick, muscular bodies shove you aside as they push out through the open gate.

After them comes the third snake, its prey in its jaws. It's sliding toward the water.

"Not so fast!" Jack shouts, and he sprints after it.

You hear a vehicle pull into the driveway and stop. Footsteps come fast around the side of the house.

Turn to page 90.

Jackson runs alongside the python that has a squirming cat in its jaws. He lifts his bat high and brings it crashing down on the snake's head.

"Come *on!*" he yells to you.

You rush over and lift your bat just as Jack smashes his down a second time. The snake is still moving.

"What's *happening* here?" a woman's voice shouts.

It's Delia from Animal Rescue.

"We *told* you!" Jack shouts. "Come on," he tells you, "hit it!"

And you do, smashing the bat down on the python's big skull. The creature just keeps moving toward the water, a bit slower but not stopping.

Jack keeps pace, slamming it again. So do you.

The snake gathers itself, and lunges toward the short bank at the back edge of the yard.

Go on to the next page.

These huge predators are so powerful, and their skulls so thick, that your bats couldn't stop this one. It slides away through the water, that poor cat now motionless in its jaws.

Breathing hard and feeling incredibly frustrated, you two stand and watch the last, splashing traces of the snake invasion settle on the water as the snake disappears. The other two snakes are already gone.

Now Delia is at your side. She's watching, too.

"Do you believe us *now*?" Jack says. He's really furious.

"How many were there?" she asks.

"Three," you say. "They got in the cage. We couldn't do anything to stop them."

She lets out a long sigh.

"This is an *invasion*," Jack tells her. He waves out at the Everglades. "What can you do to stop them?"

Turn to page 59.

The Skunk Ape lifts you, rising to its feet with you in its arms.

It carries you to a spot inside a great, thick tangle of roots and vegetation. Even though you're dazed, in shock and semi-conscious, you can tell this is some sort of hiding place.

Somehow, you know you're safe. You're very tired.

The next thing you're aware of is voices.

Someone is calling.

Calling your name.

You sit up, recognizing Jack's voice. You feel all right.

The Skunk Ape must have drawn all the venom out of you.

Before you answer Jack, you look all around.

But the creature is gone.

The End

"I'm gonna go with you," you tell Tommy. "Sorry, Jack."

Jackson's eyes are focused on Tommy's pistol. "Hey, no problem," he says.

"Don't you mess with this thing," Tommy tells him, "you hear me? The safety's on. The gun is for emergency defense *only*."

"Sure, sure," Jack says, holding the pistol up to admire it. "No problem."

You climb into the bow of the skiff. As Tommy pushes off with his pole, it glides away from shore.

"What's so odd about this bigger island?" you ask, keeping your voice very low.

"It's something we've noticed when my friends and I have gone past it, just lately," he answers softly.

You pass through the shallow water in the moonlight. The Glades at night are strange and mysterious. As Tommy poles along, you hear creatures slip into the water. You hear something paddle through the water. Flying creatures dart across the darkness above.

"Whenever people go by this island," Tommy says, "no birds rise."

Turn to page 96.

96

"In the Everglades," Tommy explains, "if your boat comes in close to any island that has trees, birds will lift up from those trees. Even if you sneak up in a little skiff like this—the birds know. And they fly."

Standing in the aft end of the skiff, Tommy dips his pole again. As he pushes off, the boat glides ahead.

"So on this island, there are lots of trees," he says, "but all of a sudden there are no birds. There has to be a reason why."

A reason occurs to you. It's chilling.

"What if this island is overrun with pythons?" you ask.

Tommy just points ahead. "On the other side of that sawgrass," he says. "That's where it is."

He poles the skiff into grass, and lets it stop. Tommy steps out of the boat.

"Careful," he warns, "sawgrass can cut you up, and there are creatures around here that are attracted by blood." He shows you how to push the grass downward, so it doesn't slice into you.

As quietly as possible, you two move through the tall, razor-sharp grass.

Go on to the next page.

After awhile, Tommy motions you to stop. He waves, and you move forward carefully.

Side by side, you two stay bent inside the grass. Tommy pushes it apart. "There it is," he says.

Ahead, across maybe 50 feet of shallow open water, is the island—and it looks as if there's no possible way in.

The edge of this island is so densely crowded with mangrove trees that it looks like a wall of jungle. The mangroves all rise above their roots, which have grown up above the water in pale, crazy tangles. If anything is in there, past those mangroves on the island, you can't see it.

"I know a way in," Tommy says. "Follow me *quietly*."

He steps out into the open water.

If there's something on the island that doesn't want you there, now you're at risk of being seen—but you have no choice. Tommy's the only one who knows where you are. You have to follow him. So you too step out from the grasses.

You move very slowly across the water.

Turn to the next page.

98

Tommy leads you into a tangle of mangrove roots that looks impenetrable. Ducking low, the young Miccosukee pushes forward.

Crouching to follow, you begin to creep into what you discover is a tunnel-like natural opening.

You hold your breath as you stumble over roots down in the water. You catch your hand on the clustered roots all around. Feeling your way forward, you're creeped out. It's dark here. What creatures' homes might you be invading?

Ahead, Tommy stops. You hear his breath catch. He motions you forward.

Go on to the next page.

Cages.

Big cages.

Four big wire cages look ghostly in the moonlight. They stand nearly five feet high and at least ten feet long, constructed from thick steel bars like the doors of prison cells.

The cages are clustered close together on a small patch of open ground that's surrounded by trees. What you're looking at is densely hemmed in, hidden from the outside world.

You see a small, dark structure, set back in those trees—but you can't see any lights or people around.

Turn to page 101.

Tommy figures it out first.

"Snakes," he hisses. "They've got a whole lot of snakes in there."

The long wire cages are filled with large, thick snakes. In the moonlight, you can just make out the big dark patches that identify them. From your online research, you know those markings.

"Burmese pythons," you whisper.

Tommy nods.

He moves his mouth close to your ear. "I don't see any people," he murmurs softly. "Do you?"

You peer around. "No."

"Someone *put* those snakes in those cages," he whispers.

You freeze.

Something is wrapping itself around your leg.

Turn to the next page.

102

You choke down a scream. Whatever's down there is twisting, curling itself around your lower left leg. And it's *moving up*.

You lurch backward, grabbing at your leg—and the sound you make causes the snakes in those cages to writhe and lurch. They're banging at the steel bars.

A light comes on.

"Get *down*," Tommy whispers—and he pushes you back into the tunnel.

That's the last direction you want to go in!

Everything inside is screaming for you to spring out of your narrow, confining hiding place—to get out where you can try to pull the creature off your leg.

If you tumble out, turn to page 103.

If you stay in the tunnel, turn to page 108.

Nothing could be worse than letting a constrictor snake wrap itself around you!

Tumbling out onto the ground, you reach back frantically, clawing at your leg. A snake has indeed wrapped itself around your right lower leg. It's not a huge snake, it looks young—and it must have mistaken your leg for a creature small enough to swallow.

You shake your leg hard. The snake's head snaps back, and it bites into your flesh.

"*OW!*"

You grab the reptile's head and yank it away from your thigh. Wrestling and rolling over, you unwrap the clenching thing, rung by rung—and now the spotlight catches you. Square on.

"Move one more inch and you're dead," says a voice.

You pull the snake's last coil from your lower leg and fling it as far as you can.

A bullet hits the ground several feet from your head.

"He's a bad shot," Tommy whispers from the tunnel. "Run for it! Get him away from those cages so I can go take a look."

"That was a warning shot!" the voice shouts again. "*Do not move!*"

If you freeze, turn to page 104.

If you run for it, turn to page 105.

You lie silent and motionless. Tommy slithers back down the tunnel. Even this close, you can't hear him go.

Footsteps approach.

"Over on your stomach," the voice orders.

The spotlight hits you full in your face. You're blinded. You turn over, onto your stomach.

The spotlight illuminates the ground beside you. A hand seizes your right wrist, twists it behind your back and holds it. You hear something else being set down.

It must be the gun.

You realize there's a split-second before the man's other hand grabs your left wrist. If you move really fast, you *might* be able to snatch the gun.

If you grab for the gun, turn to page 113.

If you don't take the chance, turn to page 120.

You leap up and run for it.

Running, you stoop to make a smaller target. You try to zigzag, like a fleeing rabbit, but the shot hits your spine with a cracking thud.

As you fall, your last thought is: *he's not a bad shot, after all.*

The End

You've got one chance. As the guard lifts your arms, you plant both feet and drive upward, as hard as you can.

"Ow! My *ear*!"

The guy hurls you to the ground. He bends over, grimacing and holding his ear.

He stoops, picks up the gun, and trains it on you.

"That was stupid," he growls. "Now I'm *mad*. Get on your feet."

He clicks off the gun's safety. "Now," he says.

Without hands to push, it's really hard—and you're so terrified you're trying hard not to cry. You're able to roll up onto your knees; you stumble to your feet.

You feel the gun barrel shoved into your back.

"Move."

He prods you over to the cage full of snakes that are only five to ten feet long. Only. There's a clinking—the gate swings open and with a rough shove, you're toppling into the cage.

"No, please! I…"

You turn just as the gate swings closed. *Click*. It's locked.

The guard walks away. "I ain't watchin' this," you hear him say. There's a rustling all around you. The snakes are coming closer. You feel the first one slide against your thigh.

Now it's climbing up your leg.

The End

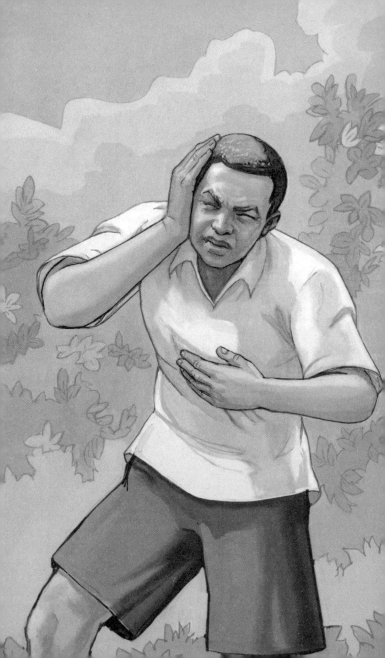

108

You duck back into the tunnel of mangrove roots. Tommy signals, placing his hand flat against his mouth, for you to be quiet.

Panic rises in your throat. It's so murky and dark that you can't really see whatever is still coiling around your leg, but you can *feel* it.

The coil is tightening.

Tommy looks toward the tunnel's opening. You realize he doesn't know what's happening to you.

You grab his shirt and yank hard. Startled, he turns.

It's too dark to see, so you take his hand, pulling it toward your leg. When Tommy's fingers touch the snake, his breath catches.

The coil is tightening. The creature thinks your leg is dinner.

If it can cut off the circulation while you two hide here in the dark, you know your leg could die.

Go on to the next page.

Tommy slides past you. "Don't move," he whispers in your ear. *"Don't move."*

You hold your breath.

Tommy works his way down until he's below you on the tunnel's vertical drop. You feel his hand grip the top of whatever's got you, and pull that part away.

Slowly, slowly, coil after coil, he pulls it off your leg.

Finally your leg is free. Tommy must still be holding the snake. You hope he's got it by the head.

"Let's get *out* of here," he whispers.

Turn to the next page.

There's no other way: you two have to cross the open water. Ahead, the sawgrass looks soft in the moonlight. If you can make it there, you can move away, crouching and hidden from anyone watching on the island.

You hear a little splash as Tommy flings the snake away. Your heart jumps into your throat, but Tommy motions with his head for you to follow him.

You push through the water. As you move, the water gurgles. Tommy, ahead, signals you to keep moving.

Turn to page 112.

Tommy makes it to the sawgrass and slips in. You follow, quickly as you can. You move a little too fast and cause a splash. Tommy glances back at the island. He waves for you to come in.

You step in, and the sawgrass closes behind you.

"What *was* that—those cages," you whisper. "What were they for?"

"I don't know," Tommy answers. "But we need to grab Jack and get *away* from here."

As you push, quietly but quickly, through the dangerous grass, you realize Tommy's probably right. You may never know why that Everglades island had four big metal cages—and why those cages were full of very large, clearly agitated snakes.

Your mind keeps asking, *Why?*

You can't even imagine what the answer could be.

The End

Your move is quick. You snatch at the pistol, but your captor is just as fast. Both your hands close on the gun. You tug as hard as you can to pull it from his grasp—but he's a grown man and he's stronger. You're about to lose the struggle, and you know it.

In a desperate move, you twist your body and thrust your knee upward with as much force as you can.

Your knee catches the guy hard in the stomach. His breath bursts out of him as he doubles over.

As he does, his hand jerks upward—and fires his gun.

Turn to the next page.

The man jerks back and drops his pistol. He's shot his own shoulder!

Adrenaline spikes through your body as you leap up and snatch the gun. Training it on the man as he writhes on the ground, you shout out: "Tommy! Tommy, he shot himself! I've got the gun!"

You hear scrambling, then running feet as Tommy joins you.

The pistol wavers in your trembling hands.

"Here," Tommy Osceola says gently. "I'll take the gun, okay?"

Go on to the next page.

"He's bleeding bad," you tell Tommy, nodding toward the man. "We should bind up his shoulder, or something."

"Right." Tommy rips a wide strip away from the base of his shirt. He winds it around the man's bleeding shoulder. Even before he's done, the bandage is soaked with blood.

"Guess I need the whole thing," Tommy says, pulling the rest of his shirt over his head.

As Tommy wraps the shirt around his wound, the man looks up at you. "You two are making a *huge* mistake," he says through teeth clenched against the pain. "You have no idea the kind of people you're dealing with here."

"We might have some idea," Tommy says. "We've met you."

"Very funny," the man says. "But I'm just a guard. When the *real* guys find out…"

"Look, shut up, okay?" Tommy tells him. "We can either take you to get help, or we can leave you here to bleed to death. Your choice."

The man curses. "I'll go," he says.

"Right," Tommy answers. Now he turns to you. "I'm…afraid you've got to stay here. For awhile."

You gulp.

"Here? By myself?" You nod toward the snake cages. "With them?"

Turn to the next page.

116

What follows is the longest hour of your life.

The normal nighttime sounds of the Everglades all around you are weird and creepy enough... but they're nothing next to the writhing, slithering tangles of thick snakes in the steel cages, just a few feet away.

You can't help flinching when the creatures bang against the steel bars. What if they get *out*?

And what if...this is even scarier...what if the people that guy was working for *do* come back? How do you know they won't?

You don't, but you have to stay. You've got no choice.

Tommy took the wounded man in the skiff. They've picked up Jack, then headed for shore. You know all this because Jack keeps you posted via text message:

**Won't be long now. We're on shore.
Heading for t's truck**

But when you hear the roar of an airboat power through the night and realize it's heading your way, you feel panic rise in your throat. Tommy didn't bring his airboat tonight...so this isn't him.

Whoever it is, they're fast.

Go on to the next page.

Jack's next text comes in:

**We're in a police boat! Got a big spotlight.
Can you see us?**

You see them.

The spotlight on the police airboat scans across the moonlit wetlands.

It's searching for you.

At last, you feel like you can breathe.

Turn to the next page.

The three police officers who brought Tommy and Jack on the airboat stand on the island puzzled, staring at the big cages. You know they must be wondering: *Why are these things filled with huge snakes?*

The cops find the little structure you spotted, back in the trees. It's a steel shed. They break its padlock, and discover sacks of reptile food, with labels from a major chain store.

So these people were *feeding* the pythons.

As dawn breaks with a rich, rosy glow over the Eastern horizon, you and Tommy Osceola watch the police as they radio for more help.

"I don't think they were just feeding those snakes," Tommy tells you. "Looks to me like they were *raising* them."

"But why? The Everglades are full of these predators," you say. "Why would anyone want to add *more*?"

Jack adds another problem. "What are the police going to do with four cages full of pythons? Except for the littler ones in that fourth cage, those snakes are huge. I mean *huge*."

"They seem to be hungry, too," Tommy observes.

It's morning now, and you're hungry. Very hungry. So you're relieved and grateful when an officer comes up and says, "Time to take you folks home."

Turn to page 129.

Your chance to grab for the gun is gone.

The man pulls your wrists together behind your back roughly, then binds them with something that holds them tight. You try to wriggle your hands, but there's no give.

It's not hopeless, you think. *He doesn't know about Tommy.*

"Stupid kid," the man mutters. "What are you *doing*, coming out here at night anyways?"

You know you'd better play along.

"I...live over in Gladeview Acres," you tell him, your head sideways on the ground. "I just like to sneak out and...you know, explore. I'm weird, I guess."

"Kid, you're not just weird," the man says as he gets to his feet. "You're about to be dead."

Go on to the next page.

With one hand, the guy reaches into his pocket and pulls out a phone.

"Got a situation here," he says into it. "Caught some kid."

He walks just out of earshot, and talks in a muffled voice. A moment later, he returns.

"Got a little bad news," he tells you. "Nobody can find out what we're doing here. They told me to feed you to the snakes."

Your heart stops.

He tries to lift you by one arm, but you go limp—he can't do it. He sets his gun down, to lift you with both hands.

Maybe now is the chance to try to escape, or is it too risky? You could keep the guy talking, and hope Tommy finds you in time.

If you try to ram your head into the guard's chin, turn to page 106.

If you try to keep him talking, turn to page 122.

122

"Sorry, kid," the man says. "Believe me, the people I'm working with—whatever they say, I do."

He gets up, and wanders over by the big cages. The gigantic snakes hit the bars with heavy smacks.

"Oh, they're hungry," the man says. "They're *really* hungry."

He comes back and squats down.

"See, the past few days, we've stopped feeding them. We're getting them ready."

You've got to stall for time—it's your only hope. Tommy Osceola is out there, somewhere.

Your face is flat against the ground. "Ready for what?" you ask.

Something tiny crawls up your lower leg. Maybe a bunch of tiny somethings, and now their stings hit you like needles of fire up your inner thigh.

"*Uhhh*," you gasp. "*Ow ow OW!*"

The man peers at your leg. He chuckles.

"Red ants," he says. "Ain't they nasty?"

Could this *possibly* get worse?

The man reaches over, and brushes the insects off your leg.

"Hey, we're not bad people," he says, as if to explain. "We're in business, that's all."

Go on to the next page.

You say, "*Business*?"

"Sure," the man says, squatting on his haunches now. He doesn't explain, just gazes at the snakes. "When we let these monsters go, they are gonna be *hungry*."

You say, "You're going to let them go?"

"We've finally got something *nobody*'s thought of before. It's *genius*."

He seems proud. *Keep him talking*, you tell yourself.

"What's genius about it?"

"See, we raised these snakes. From babies—you can buy them in Miami. Officially, they've made it illegal to import Burmese pythons, but hey—it's Florida. You can get anything here if you want it bad enough. And Florida people *love* weird reptiles."

"I believe that," you say. *Keep him talking.* "I heard a lot of people bought those snakes, then let them go when they got big."

"People can be pretty stupid—but not us," the guy says. "We've got a *plan*."

Turn to the next page.

"Okay, you've got a plan," you say. "What's so *smart* about it?"

He grins.

"We raised these things and fed them, till they were fully grown," he says. "Then, like I said, the other day we *stopped* feeding them. We want them still strong, but really *hungry*, okay?

"In a warehouse on land, we've also built up a stockpile of lab rats," he tells you. "Those are easy to get—all kinds of labs use them.

"Now those things, we've been feeding," he says, "gettin' them nice and fat. But what we haven't been doing is cleaning their cages. So now these rats are reaaaaaally *stinky*.

"Way after midnight when nobody's watching, we'll send in a couple of panel trucks that'll drop those fat, juicy, smelly rats all over that new neighborhood," he says. "The one closest to here—with all the nice, new, expensive houses."

"Gladeview Acres?"

"*That's* the one. The same time we release the rats," he says, "we open these cages."

You begin to grasp the plan. Now his grin spreads really wide.

Go on to the next page.

"What happens," the guy asks, "when people all over that nice neighborhood wake up to see huge pythons sliding through their yards? See, these snakes are gonna smell those stinky rats—and they'll go right after them."

"How do you know?" you ask, almost desperately. "Won't the snakes look for prey out here in the Everglades?"

"Kid, don't you ever watch the news? The pythons have *eaten* everything out here. There's nothing left!

"As soon as word of the snake invasion flashes around that neighborhood," he says, "everyone there'll be desperate to sell their properties. *Desperate.* And guess who swoops in and makes a bunch of low-ball offers?

"Believe me, we've got the money," he says. "Before long, we will *own* that subdivision. After the panic dies down, we put those places back on the market. We can sell them cheaper than any other properties around here, and *still* make a killing."

"You're insane," you say.

"Could be! But *you'll* never find out. See, we've got four cages here. The fourth has some younger snakes. We're still feeding those babies."

He stands up. "Tonight," he says, "we're gonna save a little money on snake food."

Turn to the next page.

The guy starts to push you toward the big cages. As he does, a shot rings out.

He drops to the ground. You stumble and fall to your knees. Blood pools around the motionless man.

Tommy Osceola bursts into the clearing, followed by a wide-eyed Jack.

Tommy turns the man over. "Got him good," he says.

Working quickly, Tommy cuts through the bindings on your wrists. Your hands tingle as blood returns to them.

"He called someone—on a cell phone," you tell Tommy. "He told them I was here."

At that moment, you hear what sounds like a small motorboat.

"It's coming up the channel," Tommy says. "Could be his people. We need to move *fast*."

A few minutes later, you three are in Tommy's skiff, hidden among sawgrass as a small powerboat, running dark with no lights, glides along a nearby channel. As it passes, you can see three men in the boat. They don't see you.

When they're well past, Tommy poles the skiff through the grass. You tell him and Jack what the men were up to. Tommy whistles.

"You can't tell anyone about this," he says.

"We can't...*tell* anyone?" you sputter. "You're kidding, right?"

Turn to page 128.

He isn't kidding.

"I shot someone back there," Tommy reminds you as he poles the skiff almost silently through the night. "Pretty sure I killed him. We have to stay as far away from this whole deal as we can. Not a word to *anyone*."

"But that guy's friends are going to lure all those pythons into my neighborhood," you say. "It'll cause a huge panic! More pets might die, too. Those monsters are *hungry*."

Tommy shrugs. "There's always going to be bad people, and they'll do bad things," he says. "We can't always fix the world."

As your darkened neighborhood looms ahead, none of you can think of what to say next.

"When the world gets out of balance," Tommy finally says, "bad things happen."

You can't think of a reason to disagree.

The End

Riding back in the airboat, you three pass two more airboats, heading your way. They're full of stern-looking authority figures in dark nylon jackets. Clearly, a bunch of law-enforcement agencies have been alerted to this strange discovery.

You wonder what they'll make of it. You wonder if anyone will figure out the mystery.

From the way that first crew told you nothing at all, you know *you'll* probably never hear an explanation.

The End

130

You can't help Jack by getting lost out there with him, so you take a deep breath, then run inside to wake up your dad. You knew he would be mad...but you didn't expect him to get *this* furious.

"You were doing *what*?" he yells, sitting up in his pajamas. "You *know* you're not allowed outside at night!"

Your little sister's bedroom door opens, and she's upset.

"What's *happening*?" she asks. "Why are you *yelling*, Daddy?"

"You see what you've done?" your dad demands of you. "Your sister hasn't been sleeping, she's been so upset about the dog—and now you've woken *her* up too!"

"Yeah, but Dad..."

It seems to take forever for you to calm them down enough to tell your dad that Jack is out there, somewhere in the swamp. When he finally understands, he leaps out of bed and you follow him outdoors.

Jack is gone. Standing at the back edge of the yard, you see no trace of him. You call and call—but there's no answer.

Go on to the next page.

You're scanning the vast Everglades. There looks to be no end to the open water out there, or to the vast patches of sawgrass growing out of it... but how far could Jack have gone? Why can't he hear you calling for him? Did he fall into deeper water...or did something gruesome and horrible happen?

Your dad rushes inside and calls the police, who send a cruiser but it can't go any further into the great wetland than you can. They radio for an airboat, a powerful flat-bottomed craft that can skim over the shallow waters and through the grasses out there.

When the boat and its crew finally arrives, they start a proper search. You're up all night, worrying and waiting, and by morning a whole team of boats, searchers, and police divers are out there, combing the Everglades.

They come back with a clue: a single one of Jack's sneakers. A search boat found it washed up at the edge of a huge stretch of sawgrass.

For two days, search parties comb those grasses, and everywhere else within several miles.

No other trace of your friend is ever found.

The End

132

"I guess we must be okay," you say. "He swam into that patch of grass."

You search and search, but there's no trace of the swimming boy.

Soaking wet and exhausted, you finally give up.

"We could see the neighborhood, back there," you say.

"I think it was this way," Jack says as he pushes carefully through some sawgrass.

And there it is. You've never been so glad to see your safe, dry home.

You two wade carefully to shore. In your yard, at the base of a palm tree, you can just make out a soft shape that seems familiar.

"Zelda!" you shout, rushing to the base of the palm.

She's nestled there, sleeping.

"Whoa—you *stink*!" you exclaim as you gently pick her up.

Whatever she's covered in coats your hands and forearms thickly. Is it snake saliva gone rancid? You can only guess—and you have no clue how she managed to get back here safely. Did she wriggle out of that snake's grip? You'll never know, and Zelda can't tell you.

But you'll forgive her for anything right now—she's made it home safe. And so have you.

Cradling your pet as she shivers in your arms, you nod goodnight to Jackson, and walk in the moonlight toward your home.

The End

ABOUT THE ARTISTS

Illustrator: Vladimir Semionov. Vladimir was born in August 1964 in the Republic of Moldavia, of the former USSR. He is a graduate of the Fine Arts Collegium in Kishinev, Moldavia as well as the Fine Arts Academy of Romania, where he majored in graphics and painting. He has had exhibitions all over the world, in places like Japan and Switzerland, and is currently art director of the SEM&BL Animacompany animation studio in Bucharest.

Cover Illustrator: Gabhor Utomo. Gabhor was born in Indonesia. He moved to California to pursue his passion in art. He received his degree from the Academy of Art University in San Francisco in Spring 2003. Since graduation, he's worked as a freelance illustrator and has illustrated a number of children's books. Gabhor lives with his wife, Dina, and his twin girls in the San Francisco Bay Area.

ABOUT THE AUTHOR

Along with nine previous Choose Your Own Adventures, **Doug Wilhelm** is the author of *The Revealers*, a young-adult novel that has been read and discussed in over 1,000 middle schools, and its sequel *True Shoes*. Doug has also written *Treasure Town*, a chapter book for younger readers published in 2016 by Pelican. He lives in Weybridge, Vermont.

**For games, activities, and other fun stuff,
or to write to Doug Wilhelm,
visit us online at CYOA.com**